CW00377022

ISLE OF THANET
THROUGH TIME
Anthony Lane

To the memory of Wilfred Booth, history teacher at Charles Dickens School, Broadstairs, his wife Pauline, daughter Ann, aged nine, and son David, aged two, whose car was crushed by a T-33 jet trainer of the United States Air Force at Manston on 9 April 1958.

AMBERLEY PUBLISHING

Fishing and farming were the main pursuits of the inhabitants of the Isle of Thanet for many centuries before sea-bathing and tourism became popular. The former remains important to Ramsgate, where over the years, numerous sailing smacks and steam drifters have served the port. Nowadays motor boats like those above still bring in substantial catches. (A.L.)

First published 2013

Amberley Publishing
The Hill, Stroud
Gloucestershire, GL5 4EP

www.amberley-books.com

Copyright © Anthony Lane, 2013

The right of Anthony Lane
to be identified as the Author of this work
has been asserted in accordance with the
Copyrights, Designs and Patents Act 1988.

ISBN 978 1 4456 0922 5

All rights reserved. No part of this book may be reprinted or reproduced or utilised in any form or by any electronic, mechanical or other means, now known or hereafter invented, including photocopying and recording, or in any information storage or retrieval system, without the permission in writing from the Publishers.

British Library Cataloguing in Publication Data.
A catalogue record for this book is available from the British Library.

Typeset in 9.5pt on 12pt Celeste.
Typesetting by Amberley Publishing.
Printed in the UK.

Introduction

Thanet was still an island at the time of the Romans but the gradual silting of the Stour and Wantsum rivers has made it part of the mainland today. After the Romans left, the inhabitants remained largely farmers and fishermen for many years, their work only interrupted by visitors as disparate as the Vikings and St Augustine.

Margate became a limb of the Cinque Port of Dover in 1229, when it had 108 inhabited houses and fifteen fishing boats. Its first harbour dated from 1320, from where sailing vessels carried barley, vegetables and fish to London.

Ramsgate became associated with Sandwich in about 1353, when the Cinque Ports Federation had its greatest influence. Development was slow, however, for a survey carried out in the time of Elizabeth I reported that the town consisted of twenty-five inhabited houses and possessed fourteen vessels of between 3 and 16 tons.

In 1736 Thomas Barber advertised a salt water bath in the basement of his New Inn at Margate, the town where in 1753 Benjamin Beale invented the first bathing machine with a modesty hood, allowing bathers to undress and take to the water in privacy. As this interest in sea bathing grew, a stream of people arrived by the sailing hoys, becoming a torrent after the entry into service of the first paddle steamship, *Thames*, in 1815. The arrival of the railway in 1846 increased this number further. In this way Margate, Broadstairs and Ramsgate became resorts, Ramsgate's harbour additionally receiving the royal patronage of King George IV, who sailed from that haven in 1821.

In writing about the Isle of Thanet I admit to a more personal involvement than has occurred in my earlier books about shipwrecks and the various Kent ports. My choice of material therefore centres more on my childhood spent in Margate. So much of what I recall from the 1950s has either been demolished or changed considerably over the last sixty years. I was fortunate to dwell in Margate during a very pleasant and relatively stable period. Most of the wartime damage was being repaired in late 1946, although some bombed sites remained which to us served as play areas. Nearly all of the private schools had survived and these and the numerous convalescent homes quickly returned to their original purposes after mainly providing billets for service personnel. The many hotels also soon regained their custom as the trains and pleasure steamers brought the visitors back to haunts they had known before the war.

Not everything was entirely tranquil. The arrival of the United States Air Force at Manston in 1950 brought events which disturbed the peaceful waters of the Thanet community. Jet fighters sometimes crashed or went out of control on the airfield, in the first case demolishing a bank and several houses in St Peters and in the second killing Mr Booth, my history teacher, his wife and children on the Ramsgate to Canterbury Road.

After the Americans left in 1958 we became more aware of rival groups among the visitors, who previously had mostly either come to sit on the beach or drink steadily in the seafront pubs.

Margate's Marine Terrace saw more than its share of mods and rockers as time went by, groups which tended to erode the reputation of a town which had not previously experienced many disruptive visitors. Cliftonville, Westbrook, Westgate and Birchington tended to relax and carry on in their own quiet way, aloof from such diversions. Broadstairs fell into this latter category as well. Chiefly known for Charles Dickens' residence and John Buchan's *Thirty-Nine Steps*, it profited from sheltered bays less easy to find as the station was inland. Remote Kingsgate had earlier its smugglers and later its schools and golf course, but it still remains one place on the island where dwellings have not been built continuously along the cliff edge.

Ramsgate prospered in the nineteenth century in the same way as Margate, developing as a sea-bathing resort and benefiting from the regular steamer service from London, it being the final port of call. Fishing remained the main occupation after the Napoleonic Wars, with a considerable fleet of smacks working from the harbour, but two world wars took a grave toll on these and the steam drifters which replaced them. Some of the latter helped to bring home a proportion of the many tired or wounded soldiers rescued from Dunkirk in 1940.

In recent years the harbour has been enlarged to accommodate cross-channel ferries, a business which has not developed as rapidly as it has at Dover, partly because for a long time there was poor road access to the port. Both Sally Line and the Belgian Railways ferries sailed from there regularly for some years, but subsequently withdrew. Nowadays TransEuropa Ferries operates regular crossings to Ostend.

Much has changed in Thanet since the 1950s. Margate has lost almost all its prestigious hotels, depressingly often to fire, the ruins being replaced by apartments. Gone also are the private schools, partly due to an improved state education system, and the few that remain usually teach English as a foreign language to students from abroad. Most serious has been the disappearance of the convalescent homes, leaving hospital patients to be discharged directly into the community. It is difficult to measure the effect on society of these losses. Margate has been deprived of coastal amenities by the ravages of the sea, churches and cinemas by bombing, and hotels and other notable buildings by the developer, the employment from those places having migrated metaphorically to the shopping town of Westwood Cross, which is now the hub of Thanet. Who remembers the Rediffusion building and Pearce Signs? Margate also has difficulty in relating to modern architecture; Ethelbert Crescent is still preserved, but it sits uneasily next to the bowling alley that replaced the Cliftonville Hotel and does not relate to the new apartments of Queen's Court. Similarly, the new Turner Contemporary gallery has more in common with the Vue multi-screen cinema complex at Westwood than the other buildings of the Parade and faces directly onto that uncertain medium, the sea.

Broadstairs and Ramsgate have fared better, having lost less. The Granville and St Cloud (now the Comfort Inn) hotel buildings still remain in roughly their original form and Wellington, Nelson and Royal Crescents all fit in well with their surroundings. Margate's jewel is the greatly improved old town, which Ramsgate cannot match, but given harbour for harbour, Ramsgate must come out the winner because of its design, the associated buildings and multitude of boats in the marina.

Having stated those concerns, Thanet still has its white cliffs, sandy beaches and sea air, qualities that drew sea bathers in the eighteenth century and still attract visitors to this day.

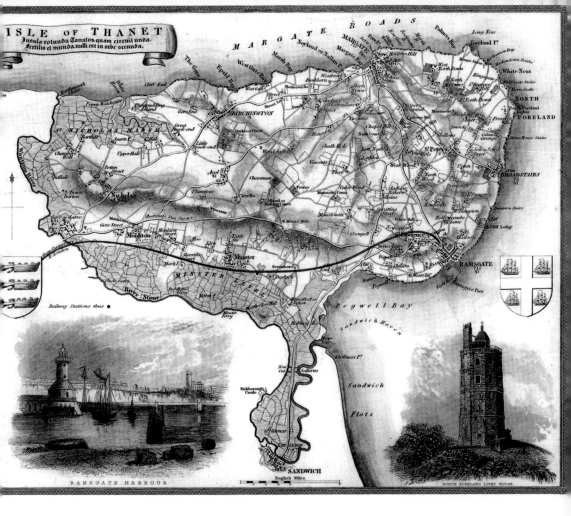

Situated at the easternmost end of Kent, some 70 miles from London, the Isle of Thanet was once separated from the mainland by the navigable Wantsum Channel, some 200 metres in width. Now reduced to a mere ditch, Thanet is an island only in name. Measuring about ten miles in length and four in width, its population has increased continuously over the years. In 1911, at the height of Edwardian enjoyment of seaside holidays, the inhabitants numbered about 65,600, while today it is estimated at 134,000, almost exactly double. The above map dates from the quieter times of 1850, long before the arrival of the motor car. Some place names have changed, but most are still recognisable. One other difference from those days is that the widespread windmills built to mill the grain have been replaced by even more turbines built offshore to generate electricity. (Thomas Moule)

Minnis Bay, which lies just to the west of Birchington, marks the start of the bays and beaches which extend via Westgate, Margate, Cliftonville, Kingsgate, Broadstairs, Ramsgate and finally to Pegwell. At the extreme end of the Thanet holiday route, it has remained somewhat quieter. The Bay Hotel, shown here, enjoyed good sea views until demolished in 1962, eventually to be replaced by apartments named Bay View Heights. (Louis Levy)

Adjoining the Bay Hotel was the famous Uncle Tom's Cabin. This was a popular venue with the young people in the fifties and sixties like St Mildred's at Westgate but sadly suffered the same fate as the hotel. (Valentine's)

I attended Woodford House School at Birchington between 1950 and 1955 when the Revd J. Douglas Ashley was headmaster. One of many private schools in Thanet, it was transferred in 1892 by H. A. Erlebach from Woodford in Essex and achieved a very sound reputation for academic achievement. Unfortunately, financial difficulties led to its closure around 1960 and demolition a year or so later. The site is now occupied by the houses of Woodford Court.

Henry Arthur Erlebach's grave, left, lies in the local churchyard. The Erlebach family ran Woodford House School until the twenties when it passed to Albert Hodges, also a well-known local figure. Close by rests the poet and artist Dante Gabriel Rossetti, right, who spent his final months in Birchington. His friend Ford Madox Brown designed the memorial (A. L.).

The building of most significance in Birchington is Quex House, which with its adjoining park is well worth a visit. The original fifteenth-century house, earlier owned by the Quekes, passed to the Powell family in the early nineteenth century. It was rebuilt in its present form around 1813, when the separate and distinctive Waterloo Tower was also constructed. The present house contains a fine collection of furniture, guns and dioramas of animals collected by Major Percy Powell-Cotton. (A. L.)

Eastward at Garlinge lies the ancient castle of Dent-de-Lion. It is believed that the Daundelyons first settled here in the time of Edward I. Later it passed to Henry Fox, Lord Holland, and before 1800 a bowling green and other 'accommodations' were open to the public. One reference describes the excellent breakfasts that were served there. Only the impressive fifteenth-century gateway remains today, surrounded by luxuriously converted barns, the whole comprising a neighbourhood watch area. (M. T. collection)

Most of the coast of Thanet has been developed to suit the needs of holiday makers and entertainment has taken a high priority. Hence numerous bandstands, concert venues and theatres were built. The Edwardian Westonville or Westbrook Pavilion was built in 1909 on the site of a former bandstand, a large amount of glazing providing a very light interior. Sadly, it was destroyed by the storm of 31 January 1953 and not replaced. (M. T. collection)

The Westbrook Pavilion was built just east of the 1791 Sea Bathing Hospital, on the promenade constructed in 1901. The site is now occupied by the colourful Strokes Adventure Golf development but still overlooked by the elegant Italianate Sea View Terrace of 1872. (A. L.)

Nearby Royal Crescent was one of a number of distinctive buildings with fine sea views constructed in Margate and Ramsgate. Earlier described as a 'stately terrace', it accommodates the Nayland Rock hotel at the eastern end. This hotel has enjoyed prosperity and decline but is once more open to guests. It is one of the few in Margate that has survived, which is an achievement in itself. (A. L.)

The multi-story Arlington House, built in 1962–3, provides a strong and unwelcome contrast with the Victorian Royal Crescent. Other interesting buildings here are the Grade II listed railway station of 1926 and the Dreamland cinema, which do relate to one another, and the interestingly named older Buenos Ayres terrace. The recent Premier Inn and the Promenade restaurant add a note of modernity. (Chris Sandwell)

The Bathing Pavilion, later Sun Deck, dating from 1926, with its enclosed pool, lay opposite Station Approach. Having changing facilities, toilets, a café and sundry stalls selling the needs of beach-goers, it replaced the individual bathing machines and tents. It was damaged in the storm of January 1978 but was left unrepaired, and not demolished until 1990. T. S. Eliot wrote the third part of his poem *The Wasteland* in the seafront shelter at right in 1921. (M. T. collection)

Another popular place of entertainment was the Hall by the Sea of 1863, which was built on Marine Terrace on the site of the LCDR terminus, alongside the Margate Sands station, and made famous by Lord George Sanger. Ward Lock's guide described as 'obtrusive' the extensive grounds, concert and ballrooms, which appear of some opulence. Dreamland cinema and amusement park later occupied this site and that of the adjacent station. (Gale and Polden)

Dreamland became very popular with visitors and the 1920 scenic railway a great attraction. 'The Caterpillar' was a rapidly rotating ride with a green hood which closed down over the riders. Dodgems and electrically powered motorboats were always fun and if you wanted to frighten the girlfriend there was always the ghost train. After many changes the park closed in 2005. A fire at the scenic railway in February 2008 caused considerable damage but it is hoped the site may one day reopen as a heritage amusement park. (M. T. collection)

Opened on 22 March 1935, the Art Deco Dreamland cinema was the largest in the town and a great attraction in its day, being close to the ballroom and amusement park. In later years it was divided into two for greater choice but this building too was closed in November 2007. Hopefully its Grade II listed status will guarantee its future. Most Thanet cinemas have been replaced by the new Vue multi-screen development at Westwood Cross. (M. T. collection)

Margate's Clock Tower was built to commemorate Queen Victoria's 1887 Golden Jubilee, the cost of £1,300 being raised by public subscription. Designed by Mr H. A. Cheers, the upper tower and clock chamber are faced with Portland stone. The part of Margate from the station to Harbour Parade was the most thronged by the visitors, and on fine days there were enormous crowds on the beach, drinking in the many bars or eating candy floss while strolling along the seafront.

Margate's oldest dwelling is the Tudor House in King Street. Originally built on a quay, documentary evidence shows that the house was already in existence by 1677 and in 1681 it was owned by Thomas Grant, a mariner of Margate. It suffered many changes over the years and was divided into three cottages by 1905. Later a victim of grave neglect, it was fortunate to receive a major restoration in 1951 that returned it to its former appearance. (C. J. Nicholas, pub. C. G. Williams, Maidstone)

Unlike the Hall by the Sea, the Assembly Rooms in Cecil Square provided entertainment for the more discerning upper classes. They were completed in about 1770, together with the nearby Theatre Royal (1787). An account of 1800 refers to masks being collected before a performance at the Assembly Rooms where, according to a plaque, King George IV met his bride when he was Prince of Wales. Sadly, the building and a fair part of the square were destroyed by fire in October 1882.

The Assembly Rooms were replaced by the Grand Theatre, which later became the Hippodrome. The Regal cinema, next door and just out of the picture to the right, became a victim of wartime bombing. Closed in 1958, the Hippodrome was pulled down together with the Regal in 1967 to make way for the new public library. This view of a very empty Cecil Square compared with the cars and crowds of today also shows the post office at left, the only Crown office left in Thanet. (M. T. collection).

The Cobbs were a very important family in Margate with interests in banking, shipping and brewing. Their brewery was built in 1807–8 by William Teanby near to the fort and gradually extended over the years. Rival Whitbread finally bought out the firm in 1968, afterwards demolishing the brewery. The above print shows the site early in the nineteenth century. (J. Shury)

This selection of labels from Cobb's beers shows considerable variety. Nut Brown Ale and Four Star Ale were further products. Forty-two tied public houses also passed to Whitbread ownership at the time of the sale.

This picture by a beach photographer shows a group of ladies enjoying themselves in the 1920s or thereabouts. The absence of any oars or other means of propulsion suggests the boat was used only to give a maritime theme to the picture and not for a voyage afloat. Many such pictures were taken to provide holiday makers with a souvenir of their stay. (A. H. Remington-Photosnaps, Westonville)

A perennial attraction to the younger members of visiting families was the donkey ride. This group are enjoying the occasion on the Marine Sands at Margate in the mid-seventies but the same could be said of children 100 years earlier. A more unusual arrival on the seafront was a petrol-driven mechanical elephant which offered rides for a season or so. (A. L.)

Until the arrival of the railway, travellers to Margate in the nineteenth century most often arrived by sea, initially by sailing hoys and after 1815 by paddle steamer. The trip was not always comfortable, as can be imagined from this picture, as the harbour was exposed to north-westerly winds and the voyage under sail could often take two days. Even in August 1905, 'Maud' wrote, 'Got down here alright on Sunday after having been seven hours on the water. It was very windy and awfully cold – the weather is rotten – hope it will soon change.'

On a fine day with a breeze there was often nothing more stimulating than sailing on the water. Boats such as the *Moss Rose*, shown here with 6-foot 8-inch Albert Emptage at the helm, and the *Sunbeam* provided an hour's trip for sixpence (2½ pence) in Edwardian times. However, on bad days, such a voyage was often referred to as a 'sixpenny sicker'. (M. T. collection)

Margate Harbour became much busier with the advent of the paddle steamer in 1815 and it was in that year that John Rennie completed the stone pier. These two views show the latter from different angles. This artist's impression made from the fort dates from 1823. (W. Daniell)

This later engraving of around 1840 shows the 1828 cast iron archway providing an entrance to Jarvis' wooden landing stage, constructed in 1824, at extreme right and the rather fine Droit House, completed in 1828 as the office of the Margate Pier & Harbour Company, in the foreground. A line of lamp standards also provides illumination. (Tallis)

Jarvis' landing stage was replaced over the years 1853–6 by an iron high-water landing stage, known as the Jetty to avoid confusion with the stone pier. It was the first built by engineer Eugenius Birch, who later gained fame for creating piers at other resorts. At 1,240 feet, it was 120 feet longer than Jarvis' stage. This artist's impression was created in 1853. (*Illustrated London News*)

A hexagonal head was added to the Jetty between 1875 and 1877 at a cost close to £35,000. It provided space for a bandstand, shelters, six kiosks and the grand pier pavilion shown above. Admission to this jetty head cost two pence. A drifting vessel severed the jetty in 1877 and a fire ravaged the head in November 1964 but in its day it was a great institution. Classed as unsafe and closed in 1974, the structure was almost totally destroyed by the gale of January 1978. (M. T. collection)

BELLE STEAMERS,

Special Cheap Trip
(Weather and other circumstances permitting)
BY THE SALOON STEAMER,
Woolwich Belle
Friday, 14th September,

To MARGATE
AND BACK,
Leaving Walton 10.15, Clacton 10.45,

Allowing about **2 hours** ashore
And returning from Margate 3.30 p.m.
RETURN SALOON FARES:

FROM WALTON
OR CLACTON, **3/6**

CHILDREN HALF-PRICE,
Tickets available day of issue only,

Further particulars may be obtained of the Pier-
masters at Clacton and Walton.

Numerous steamers brought visitors to Margate over the years between 1815 and 1966. The main contenders in late Victorian and Edwardian times were the General Steam Navigation Company (GSNC) and Belle Steamers. An interesting cross-estuary trip from Walton and Clacton is advertised by the latter at left, while at right is pictured Captain J. Hall of the *Southend Belle*. (*Belle Steamers Guide*, 1914)

The *Southend Belle* enjoyed a long life under various owners. Built by Wm Denny of Dumbarton in 1896, her triple expansion engines gave her a speed of up to 18 knots. After the First World War she worked mainly to Essex resorts. Renamed *Laguna Belle* in 1929, she passed in 1935 to the GSNC, who kept her till the later war, when she served as minesweeper HMPMS 532. Afterwards unfit for reconditioning, she was broken up in 1946. (Belle Steamers)

MAGNIFICENT SALOON STEAMER

ROYAL SOVEREIGN

FIRST SAILING, SATURDAY, JUNE 5th, 1926

TO

SOUTHEND, MARGATE and RAMSGATE

TIMES: (Weather & other circumstances permitting)

DAILY (Fridays Excepted) LEAVING:		RETURNING FROM:	
OLD SWAN PIER (London Bridge)	8.30 a.m.	RAMSGATE	2.5 p.m.
GREENWICH	9.0 "	MARGATE	2.45 "
NORTH WOOLWICH	9.30 "	SOUTHEND	4.40 "
SOUTHEND	11.20 "	NORTH WOOLWICH (arrive about)	6.40 "
MARGATE	1.20 p.m.	OLD SWAN PIER (London Bridge)	7.40 "
RAMSGATE (arrive about)	2.0 "		

FARES (SEASON)

From Old Swan Pier, Greenwich or North Woolwich.

Southend		Margate		Ramsgate	
SINGLE	RETURN	SINGLE	RETURN	SINGLE	RETURN
3/-	5/-	6/-	10/-	6/6	11/-

CHEAP DAY RETURNS

On Mondays, Tuesdays, Wednesdays & Thursdays (Except Bank Holidays).

Southend 4/6   Margate 8/-   Ramsgate 9/-

BOOK IN ADVANCE.

LONDON BRIDGE: 7, Swan Lane and 40a, King William Street, E.C.4
Telephone Central 9220

GREENWICH & WOOLWICH PIER Booking Offices and J.W. ANDREWS, 29 London Street, Greenwich.

A very popular steamer on the London to Margate and Ramsgate run was the *Royal Sovereign*, built by Fairfields in 1893. She was 300 feet in length and of 891 gross tons. Initially operated by the Victoria Steamboat Association, she ran continuously until the First World War with her near-sister *Koh-I-Noor*. This poster gives her sailings for 1926, close to the end of her service. (Margate Museum)

PS *Royal Sovereign* seen approaching Margate. In 1918 the vessel was sold to the Royal Sovereign Steamship Co., and in 1929 she was bought by General Steam who ran her only for that season, when she made fifty-six trips between London and Margate. Having the capacity for some 1,400 passengers, it was estimated that she had carried around 2 million to the Kent resorts during her lifetime. (C.U.D.O.)

Nowadays the *Royal Sovereign*'s trips down the Thames are repeated once or twice annually by the preserved paddle steamer *Waverley*, seen at Margate in October 2010. As the jetty was dismantled after the 1978 storm she has to moor at the stone pier head, a more difficult situation with less water. (A. L.)

The last of the paddle steamers on the Margate run, and the largest, was the *Royal Eagle*, built by Cammell Laird at Birkenhead in 1932. She was luxuriously fitted out, having a promenade deck with observation lounges and a sun deck above.

A series of postcards were produced for the *Royal Eagle* This one shows the main dining saloon. In total 322 diners could be accommodated in her saloons, where 'excellent breakfasts, luncheons and teas at very moderate prices were served, the steamers being fully licensed'. Her popularity was short-lived, however, for the war soon intervened and the new motor ships took over in the peacetime which followed, leaving her in a supporting role. She was broken up in 1953. (G.S.N.C.)

The second of the General Steam motor ships was the *Royal Daffodil* of 1939. Their white hulls and streamlined features were a far cry from the paddle steamers. Wm Denny were once more the builders and the *Daffodil* of 2,060 gross tons achieved 21 knots with two sets of 12-cylinder diesels. Her passenger license allowed for 2,073 passengers to be carried. (G.S.N.C.)

Bob Marsh from Ramsgate was the *Royal Daffodil's* announcer in 1962. After the war the ship made cruises to view the French coast on Sundays, Tuesdays, Wednesdays and Saturdays after sailing from Gravesend and calling at Southend and Margate. On Mondays and Thursdays she sailed along the English coast off Dover and Folkestone, a pattern which continued until 1956, when landing restrictions were lifted and 'no passport' trips to the French ports permitted. These were made mostly by the *Queen of the Channel.* General Steam's Thames services ceased completely at the end of 1966, with the *Daffodil* going to Belgian breakers the following year.

Returning to the Jetty and looking towards the land, this engraving of May 1868 shows from the left, Holy Trinity church, Cobb's Brewery, the Sailor's Observatory, the Pier and Duke's Head Hotel – which were replaced by the Metropole Hotel – and finally the Droit House at far right. The cliffs to the east of the jetty were to become the site of the Marine Palace. (Rock & Co.)

In 1875 the Margate Skating Rink and Aquarium Company planned the construction of the grandiose Marine Palace on a reclaimed area beneath the cliffs shown above. By 1884 it comprised of a skating rink, three-story restaurant, separate ladies' and men's swimming baths, a theatre, ballroom and switchback railway. It prospered greatly but inadequate sea defences and flimsy construction led to its almost total destruction in the storm of November 1897. (*Penny Illustrated Paper*)

This Edwardian view of the Harbour Parade contains a wealth of interest. Trams and horse-drawn carriages provide the only means of transport. Numerous wherries crowd the harbour slipway, many of them for hire. Cobb's Ship Hotel lies at the entrance to the jetty and a poster next door advertises, '*News of the World*, Largest and Best Sunday Paper, 1d!' Meanwhile the small paddler *Conqueror* leaves the Jetty head on a local excursion. (Rapid Photo)

The White Hart and Royal York Hôtel. — LL.

This different view of the Harbour Parade shows the well-known White Hart Hotel at left and the adjoining Royal York Hotel. Out of sight to the left are the Parade, later Classic cinema and the Benjamin Beale pub, previously the Hoy Hotel. Today the White Hart has been replaced by modern apartments while the building at right survives as Royal York Mansions. (Louis Levy)

In contrast to today, Margate's harbour was very busy in the past. This typical scene shows a sailing barge alongside the stone pier and a number of shrimping bawleys moored to buoys. Spritsail barges would carry cargoes as diverse as coal, grain and beer, while the tank barge *Hydrogen* would take away coal tar produced by the local gasworks.

F. T. Everard obtained the contract to supply the gas works with coal in about 1925 and had four steel sailing barges built for the purpose, the *Alf, Ethel, Fred* and *Will Everard*. The firm's motor coasters gradually replaced them and here a steam crane unloads the MV *Accruity* in the fifties while fascinated youngsters and those not so young look on. (M. T. collection)

A further view of the Jetty head with the PS *Conqueror* leaving for an excursion. The Jetty is as busy as always but the numerous warships anchored in Margate Roads add an extra dimension and a reminder that the First World War is not far away. Visible also are Margate's two pulling and sailing RNLI lifeboats, the *Eliza Harriett* and *Civil Service No. 1*, stationed on slipways at either side of the Jetty. Later a boathouse was built on the east slipway, here occupied by *Civil Service No. 1*. (Bobby & Co.)

In contrast, nowadays Margate's lifeboat is housed in the area previously occupied by the Marine Palace and east of the new Turner Contemporary. There has been no slipway since the collapse of the Jetty and the boat is now launched by tractor from the beach, as shown here in September 2000 for the Mersey relief boat *Peggy and Alex Caird*. (A. L.)

The 1891 Metropole Hotel enjoyed a prominent position close to the entrance to the Jetty. Next door to its right was the Ship Hotel, with the Camera Obscura in front. Unwelcome fame reached the Metropole in October 1929 when Sidney Fox murdered his mother in room 66 before setting it on fire. All of these buildings and those nearby such as the Sailor's Observatory were swept away by the construction of the Fort Hill dual carriageway in 1938–9 and the war that followed. Nothing in this view remains today. (Louis Levy)

The Rendezvous area occupied by the above buildings was chosen some years ago for the site of the new Turner Contemporary gallery. Whether this was wise or not only time will tell. Certainly it provides a great contrast with the other buildings in the vicinity and the nearby Old Town cafés and boutiques which have improved in recent years. (A. L.)

There was considerable naval activity off Margate in the Edwardian years, some involving searchlight practice, which could be impressive when numerous warships were anchored in the Roads. Heavy guns could also often be heard from Shoeburyness on the other side of the Thames, sounds which can still be heard today. Warships still visited Margate in the 1950s, including the minesweeper HMS *Cheerful*, mine-layer HMS *Apollo* and aircraft carrier HMS *Ocean*. (S. Hildesheimer & Co.)

Margate is no exception in enjoying a variety of weather. In the severe winter of 1963 the sea froze for some distance offshore, creating Arctic conditions, but by this time the harbour was not often used commercially, trade being confined to barges carrying aggregate. (S. A. Lane)

Strong north-easterly winds cause heavy seas to break along the shoreline and over the pier. Extended promenades have much reduced the regular toll of cafés and bathing establishments lost to winter storms in the past. Most of northern Thanet is now defended in this way, except for a section at Birchington. (A. L.)

The Fort, Margate

The hill immediately to the east of the harbour has long been known as Fort Point or the Fort, but does not seem to have been extensively fortified, except perhaps in Napoleonic times. Security was provided locally by the Coast Blockade officers, later the Coastguards, who had stations at 2-mile intervals, the nearest being at Newgate Gap. (Valentine's)

The Fort, Margate

This view in the opposite direction to the last picture shows Fort Crescent and the Fort bandstand of 1865 in more detail. A carnival procession appears to be in progress. The message on the back of the card reads, 'Dear F., Time flies too quickly here – was never in a place I like so much.' (Valentine's)

The bandstand above was removed to further along the Queen's Promenade to allow the construction of the specially landscaped Pavilion and Winter Gardens, opened in August 1911. Various additions were made later, including the post-war Sun Lounge, a second smaller theatre, which became the Queen's Hall in 1965. The Winter Gardens has offered a wide variety of entertainment over the years, including boxing and wrestling matches, orchestral concerts and performances by the Beatles and Chippendales. (A. L.)

Margate's Winter Gardens was only one of the many places of entertainment. The Hall by the Sea, Hippodrome, Westbrook Pavilion, Jetty Pavilion, numerous bandstands and Lido Theatre all needed talent to entertain the masses. German bands, pierrots, minstrels, troubadours and concert parties all had their periods of popularity. This photo of Gee's Troubadours dates from 1909. (M. T. collection)

Ladies were by no means absent, for Jessie Wildon and her band are represented here. Her husband Jack also toured with a group of musicians. After the last war Ivy Benson came to Margate with her band. Nearly all the famous names visited Thanet to perform, particularly the comedians. (M. T. collection)

A fine, new promenade was also laid to the seaward side when the Winter Gardens was built and, in this Edwardian scene, the Fort Paragon Hotel can be seen on the cliff above the rear of the Pavilion. (Photochrom Co., Celesque)

There were also numerous sea bathing establishments around the town in the nineteenth century. Clifton Baths were established in about 1824 on the site that became the Lido. By 1829, the date of this engraving, water pumped to a higher level by horses maintained hot baths, while below the normal cold sea water variety were available. Separated facilities for gentlemen and ladies provided seven hot baths, showers and hip baths. Other diversions included a reading room and newsroom equipped with organ and billiard table. (G. Shepherd-McClatchie)

It was not until 1927 that this large, outdoor swimming pool was built. The site, which in 1938 became the Lido, had full changing facilities, bars, a theatre and open-air stage. Many bathing beauty competitions were held by the pool. It was immediately recognisable by the chimney placed directly at the bottom of Ethelbert Road so as not to interrupt the view from adjacent hotels. This later carried large illuminated signs indicating the Lido. (H. & S. Series, Margate)

A heavy sea in May 1996 recreates the illusion of the swimming pool but sadly it has been filled with rubble and topped with concrete. The changing rooms, adjoining facilities and features of the earlier baths are now closed off and derelict but some parts of the site are listed. The Golden Garter Saloon is still standing but the theatre and Jamaica Inn have gone. (A. L.)

35

The Cliftonville Hotel, built in Ethelbert Crescent in 1868, was one of the most prestigious in Thanet. Owned by the Gordon Hotels Co., it offered boarding terms from 5 guineas per week in 1920, a considerable sum indeed. There was also a motor garage. As was the fate of so many others, it suffered a major fire in March 1952 and was demolished ten years later to be replaced by more modern necessities: a bowling alley, night club and apartments. (The Thanet Series)

Clients arrive by carriage at the door of the Cliftonville Hotel in 1911. Many famous guests must have stayed there, given the importance of the resort in the Victorian and Edwardian eras. The nearest way to the sea was via Newgate Gap, a short distance to the east.

There was originally a Coastguard post at Newgate, which may have been the reason for creating the gap. Known earlier as 'Devil's' Gap, I remember that as a child it made me feel strangely uncomfortable. It was bridged over in 1856–61 by Captain Hodges to provide a continuous promenade to his cannon and flagstaff at Palmer's (later Palm) Bay, where refreshments were available. (Nelson Morgan, Stationer, Margate)

The earlier 42-foot iron bridge was replaced by this tiled version in 1907, built to commemorate the jubilee of the incorporation of the Borough of Margate in 1857. There were many attractions on the beach below the gap, including donkey rides for children and Charlotte Pettman's 'Original Sea Water Baths', with their long platform leading to bathing machines and a line of dressing boxes. (A. L)

37

This steel girder bridge had endured eighty years when water penetration caused severe damage to the interior concrete and it became unsafe, eventually to be closed to the public. It was replaced by a simpler brick-and-steel structure in 2003.

Looking inland from the bridge over Newgate Gap, the Queen's and Highcliffe hotels lie on the eastern side in the delightful Queen's Gardens. The handsome road viaduct with its artificial rock decoration is also visible at right. (The Thanet Series)

They were eventually combined to form the Queen's Highcliffe Hotel, with the addition of a central tower in 1911. In 1955, Billy Butlin bought this and the nearby Norfolk, St Georges, Grand and Florence hotels. After a fire in the tower, that area, including the indoor swimming pool, was converted into a Dolphinarium, quite an innovation for its day. (WHS Kingsway Real Photo)

John Betjeman wrote about Margate while staying at the Queen's Highcliffe in 1940 but this did not assure it any protection. It lasted longer than the Cliftonville, but once Butlins withdrew, it was the first to go. The Queen's Court apartment complex now occupies the site. (A. L.)

Just around the corner on the Eastern Esplanade, situated opposite the Oval bandstand, was the Cliftonville Hydro Hotel, built in 1899. One attraction of this establishment was the Turkish baths. In 1920 it was renamed the Grand and much later given new life by Billy Butlin but it has also been replaced by apartments. (Valentine's)

A little further along the Esplanade, the St Georges Hotel had a parallel later history. It was linked with the Norfolk and Grand by a subterranean passageway, the three providing 254 rooms in total. Butlins sold all three in 1999, but that was almost the end of the story, the Norfolk and Grand being demolished in 2005 and the St Georges in 2010, remaining at the moment an empty site. The Florence, dating from 1912–3, and Darwin Court, the Norfolk's replacement, are also apartments. (Butlins)

The sole survivor of the larger Cliftonville hotels is the Walpole Bay, in Fifth Avenue, built for Louisa Budge in 1914 and extended in 1927. The Otis lift is of the latter date and the hotel generally tries to recapture the past by retaining a collection of artefacts and memorabilia. It has thirty-seven en-suite rooms, most with balconies. The glazed veranda at the front affords an excellent place to take afternoon tea. (A. L.)

Most of the bathing facilities have disappeared but there remain, in several places, pools such as this at Walpole Bay where water is retained once the tide has gone out. As children we spent a lot of time here, and I remember one lad who dived in wearing the shorts his mother had knitted and who kicked away what he thought was seaweed between his legs. Only on emerging did he find he was separated from his shorts, which had sunk without trace. (A. L.)

The Bungalow & Flagstaff Parade, Cliftonville.

J.W.S. 3412.

Just beyond the Walpole Bay Hotel lies another gap-way, the final hurdle en route to Hodges Flagstaff (far left) and the Koh-I-Noor Café (right), later the Bungalow Café. Earlier known as Jesus' Gap, it was re-christened Hodges Gap when the well-known captain provided a bridge. This also was replaced in 1907 and again in 1993. (I. Welch & Sons)

The same area seen in 2011, with the new bridge and gap closer to the foreground. Nearest building is the coastguard lookout, which is also a base for the Margate Cliff Rescue Team. The extensive and once very popular Bungalow Café area beyond is now occupied by the Bethesda Medical Centre. (A. L.)

The beach cafés were equally popular in their day, having developed from the bathing stations. These two illustrations are of successive buildings at Palm Bay, last but one of the Cliftonville bays and served by Sackett's Gap. This one was demolished by violent winter gales around 1949.

A replacement was constructed which fared somewhat better but as these buildings faced northward they were always exposed to bad weather, especially in winter. There was a similar one to this at Walpole Bay but both were lost by 1980. The building at centre rear is Godwin Girls' School, referred to later. (St Alban's Series)

Trinity Church, Margate

Hotels and theatres were not the only buildings to suffer disaster in Thanet. Holy Trinity church, which occupied a conspicuous position in Trinity Square above the harbour, was a lofty structure dating from 1829. It became a victim of a German high explosive bomb on 1 June 1943 but the walls and tower remained standing until 1961. The gardens to the south, including the war memorials, have survived but the area earlier occupied by the church is now a car park. (Valentine's)

A new Holy Trinity church was commenced close to Northdown Park, adjoining St Mary's Chapel, in 1957. Besides normal services, this popular church has a number of different youth groups and evangelical outreach activities. Refreshments are served daily to passers by. (A. L.)

Another wartime casualty was the Astoria cinema, situated at the junction of Northdown Road with Wyndham Avenue. Built in the Art Deco style, it was opened by Jessie Matthews and Sonnie Hale in August 1934. Probably the shortest-lived of Margate's cinemas, it was closed after being bombed in July 1940. The Cameo, only a short distance from the Astoria in Northdown Road, was closed in 1969 and demolished the following year. (M. T. Collection)

A cinema with a much longer history is the Carlton at Westgate, constructed originally in 1910 as the Westgate Town Hall in a Swiss Gothic style. It was never used as such but became a skating rink. In 1912 it became the Town Hall cinema, a name which it held until 1932 when it was altered to the Carlton. Converted to three screens in recent years, this survivor is now celebrating 100 years as a cinema. (A. L.)

My parents and maternal grandparents moved to White Lodge in Laleham Road in 1947. It was, I believe, the first house built in the road in around 1914, and, as this early picture shows, there was open farmland as far as Northdown Way. There were still bomb-scarred fields to the rear and Cliftonville School's playing field to the front at the time of our arrival, but within about fifteen years most had been built on. (S. A. Lane)

NORTHDOWN, CLIFTONVILLE

The junction of Northdown Way with Northdown Park Road, seen at a similar date to the above picture. The Thanet Electric Tramway service began in 1901, starting from Westbrook and running along the seafront to Cliftonville, then Northdown and across the fields to St Peters, Broadstairs and Ramsgate. Very popular in their day, the trams were eventually withdrawn on 27 March 1937. (Valentine's)

Urban development inevitably spreads outwards. In 1963 the fourteen-storey Invicta House was completed between Laleham Road and Northdown Way. While not of great architectural merit, it did afford a means of viewing the locality not available before. This view towards the east shows Northdown Park in the distance and the new St Anthony's School and houses of Biddenden Close in the foreground. (A. L.)

A view to the north from Invicta House, with buildings of interest marked. The Montrose and Laleham School buildings have survived, still devoted to educational purposes, but house construction is already well advanced on the Cliftonville School site in the foreground in this 1965 picture. Martin Walter's garage was taken over by Invicta Motors but later demolished. The site is now occupied by Queen Elizabeth Lodge. (A. L.)

ESTD. OVER 60 YEARS   PHONE 137

Godwin Girls' College

GOOD MODERN EDUCATION

Preparation for all Examinations

Music a speciality.   Large Playing Field.   All Sports.

Individual Care.   :   Fees moderate and inclusive.

Specially-built new and up-to-date School premises, including gymnasium, on the magnificent Palm Bay Estate overlooking the Sea.

Principal :   Miss BENNET, Med. Singing, L.A.M.

(PUPIL OF SIGNOR ALBERT VISETTI)

Palm Bay, Cliftonville, Margate

One example of the many private schools in Thanet in the post-war years was Godwin Girls' College, situated in a prominent position overlooking Palm Bay. There are very few of these institutions today as the state system improved to cater for most children's needs. One exception is the Royal School for the Deaf on Victoria Road, which came to Margate in 1875 and which has recently been completely rebuilt and modernised. (*Kelly's Thanet Directory*)

The Godwin Girls' building has survived and, converted into apartments, now rejoices in the name of Goodwin Court. It was occupied by RAF personnel who worked at the Foreness radar station during the last war. (A. L.)

PALM BAY
GARAGE
Northdown Road,
Cliftonville

MOSCOW 1500 m.s.   GREENLAND 1350 m
MONTE CARLO   OLDE CHARLES ½ m

TAXI!
PHONE
MARGATE
919

GARAGE

PALM BAY GA   BP
ETHYL

My father Sam Lane worked as manager at Palm Bay Garage, Cliftonville, having moved from Leicestershire in 1946 with owners Les Brown and Harry Tooke. He also drove one of the taxis, an ex-army staff car, HKP 356, shown at left. This early post-war view of the garage shows the rather unusual signpost which the town council required removed after a complaint by a visitor about 'misleading information'. (Palm Bay Garage)

Driving was still an adventure in those days, particularly in the winter of 1947. By way of contrast to the Vauxhall 25 HP taxi in which I was sometimes allowed to travel, our own Morris was a simple affair. My photograph at left, with friend John Chamberlain, was taken with Thanet's extensive cornfields in the background in the early fifties. More formally, at right I am sporting the new design of maroon blazer with light-blue stripes required by Woodford House School in 1953. (S. A. Lane)

Palm Bay Garage eventually obtained a Ford dealership but owing to reorganisation lost out to Invicta Motors and so had to look for an alternative. They were approached by Toyota but thought a Japanese name would not catch on and so were accepted by Renault instead. Proudly showing off his new Renault 16 is comedian Hugh Lloyd, who was starring at the Winter Gardens. Sadly, the garage closed towards the end of 2012. (S. A. Lane)

Piano-smashing competitions became popular in the sixties, but to go one better the Margate and District Car Club organised a car-smashing competition where all components had to be passed through a roughly 2-foot-square frame. Members pose around this Standard in a field near Richborough power station before the start. (A. L.)

Still retaining the transport theme but returning briefly to bathing, three young ladies pose on the steps of their horse-drawn bathing machine before entering the water. Their Edwardian costumes are hardly flattering, but usually men wore nothing at all, and hence were separated. At right, a model poses for members of the Isle of Thanet Photographic Society about sixty years later. (M. T. collection – S. A. Lane)

Farming having played such an important part in Thanet's history, barley, potatoes and cauliflowers were until recently the main crops, but by way of a difference, a combine harvests grass seed at Bill Sayer's Cleeve Court Farm, Acol, in the summer of 1966. The grass was first mown then allowed to dry for some days before being picked up by Alf Bedwell on this machine. The fellow filling the sack at rear had no way of avoiding the all-penetrating dust. (A. L.)

Loading sacks of grass seed on to a trailer at Cleeve Court. Each weighed around 2 cwt and needed careful handling. Eric Ling, on the trailer, and his brother Dick both had a physique that allowed them to lift and stow the sacks with apparently little effort. We youngsters were only too glad of the petrol-powered elevator. (A. L.)

Present-day farming of a different kind. Large areas of land on what was Monkton Road Farm nearby have now been placed under glass in a massive project known as Thanet Earth. Tomatoes, peppers and cucumbers are grown above ground in these huge greenhouses using hydroponics as a system of regulating feed to the roots. Carbon dioxide is also recycled as part of this nutritive process. (Thanet Earth)

On returning to the coast, a series of arches could be found, moving south-eastwards from Margate towards Broadstairs. The first, at left, was at Botany Bay, near Kingsgate. A victim of chalk cliff erosion, it fell in the late 1960s, leaving a stack. The second, right, was the Smuggler's or Old Cutting Gap at Kingsgate close to the Captain Digby pub, the upper part of which fell in just before the last war, leaving a normal gap with a history! It was used by the local lifeboat between 1862 and 1897. (A. L., Valentine's)

The only one remaining is the man-made flint arch of York Gate in Harbour Street, Broadstairs, apparently built by George Culmer in about 1540, when it had heavy doors beneath that could be closed if there was a threat of invasion. (E. S.)

North Foreland lighthouse near Broadstairs, with its companion at South Foreland, originally guided mariners clear of the dangerous Goodwin Sands and into the Thames. Built of brick and flint, the base of the tower dates from 1691; the upper storey from 100 years later. It was rendered over in Victorian times. North Foreland was the last Trinity House station to be automated in November 1998, and all remaining keepers left the service on that date. (A. L.)

This plaque commemorates the automation ceremony. In years gone by, many visitors would climb the lighthouse and listen to the anecdotes of the keepers before seeking some refreshments in the Dutch Tea House opposite but since automation the 85-foot tower has rarely been opened to the public. Nowadays the keepers' dwellings are available as luxurious holiday lets. (A. L. – Valentine's)

Engineer Thomas Crampton's water-tower close to Broadstairs Broadway is another flint building of note. An inventor and locomotive engineer of some renown, Crampton (1816–88) grew up in Broadstairs and later also built the bridge over Louisa Gap, named after his daughter. Part of the 1859 waterworks, this tower was eventually superseded by the one in Rumfields Road, below. It now houses a museum devoted to its builder. (A. L.)

Springs were found in Rumfields Road early in the last century. In 1925 this water-tower was built by Broadstairs and St Peters Urban District Council to contain the water pumped to the surface. Constructed of ferro-concrete, the tower cost £25,650 and at that time was able to contain 250,000 gallons of water, while a further 300,000 gallons could be held in a reservoir at ground level. Nowadays the site is owned and operated by Southern Water, who pump in extra water from the Fleete Reservoir. (A. L.)

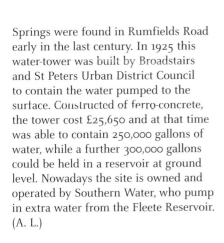

Fort House, which overlooks Broadstairs Harbour, was Charles Dickens' favourite home during the period 1840–70. It dates from the early years of the nineteenth century and remained in this form until 1901, when a new wing was added and the whole house largely rebuilt in a castellated form. It was around that time it was rechristened 'Bleak House' after Dickens' novel of 1852. (The Photochrom Co.)

The present shape of Bleak House is apparent at the rear of this Edwardian view of Broadstairs Harbour, which shows the old and still prominent Tartar Frigate inn at centre. The wooden pier-master's office at right is decorated with figureheads and other maritime memorabilia, an example of which is shown in the next illustration. (Louis Levy)

It is likely that this Scotsman came from the barque *Highland Chief*, wrecked on the Goodwin Sands on 12 February 1869. Eleven hands were saved when the ship broke up, but figureheads often also survived these disasters. There are additionally two whale rib bones from a specimen cast ashore in 1762 and a figurehead believed to be Hercules. (A. L.)

Looking towards the pier head, the lifeboat can be seen drawn up on its slipway at left. The RNLI, however, closed the station in 1912. Dickens described the much-tarred pier, which dates mostly from 1808, as 'fortunately without the slightest pretension to architecture and very picturesque in consequence'. Somewhat later, seats were placed at the end and a large awning arranged overhead. (JWS)

Given the numerous shipwrecks that occurred on the notorious Goodwin Sands and coastal areas nearby, few casualties occurred at Broadstairs. Crowds therefore thronged the shore on 11 November 1962 when the broken-down French trawler *Jean Pierre et Phillippe*, B.2737, was driven by a gale into Viking Bay, the crew being rescued by breeches buoy. The ship was later broken up on the beach. (John G. Callis)

A recent view of Viking Bay on a summer's day. Again the beach is crowded with people, for Broadstairs remains a popular spot, but this time there is not the urgency related to the above, when the coastguards reported, 'Everybody on the pier where we rigged our equipment was willing to lend a hand and even some women were hauling on the line to bring the crew ashore.' (A. L.)

Main Bay, Broadstairs, seen in earlier times. Gone are Wilson's Public Bathing Tents and associated Tea Room, where it was possible to obtain light refreshments, teas, ices and American iced drinks. Eagle House at left, however, still remains. It was earlier the headquarters of the Coast Blockade and was the first place in England to learn of Wellington's victory at Waterloo, the captured French eagle standards being brought there. Main Bay became Viking Bay after the arrival of the Viking ship *Hugin* in 1949. (J. Welch & Sons)

A much greater range of seashore entertainment is available in Viking Bay today, including swings, slides, trampolines and a bouncy castle or rather giraffe. It is difficult to know what the Victorians would have thought of these diversions but there remains an element of nostalgia in this picture with the presence of the sailing barge *Lady of the Lea* in the harbour. (A. L.)

Away from the antiquity of the harbour, and in sharp contrast, the local education authority built two new, well-designed schools at Broadstairs in the fifties: the secondary modern, Charles Dickens School, shown new here in 1955, and the nearby Dane Court technical school a little later. They filled a large gap in local educational needs, both for moderate achievers and those with technical ambitions.

Charles Dickens School prefects pose for a photograph with headmaster Leslie Warren in the summer of 1956. The front row comprises from left, if my memory serves me correctly: Dawn Harwood, Angela Bushell, Patricia Hann, Maureen Childs, the author, David Walker, Neil Murrell and Graham Noble. (Sunbeam Photo Ltd)

While St George's new school buildings appear in the background to this 1996 photograph, interest lies in the rather forlorn North Foreland Radio Station in the foreground which, with the call sign GNF, handled all ship-to-shore radio traffic, including 2182 kHz distress messages, for south-east England. It was moved to 96 Rumfields Road from a location near North Foreland lighthouse in 1923 and closed in 1991. An ASDA supermarket now occupies the site. (A. L.)

The Home for Convalescent Children of the Better Class established by shipbuilder Sir Alfred Yarrow at Broadstairs in 1894 is of much more architectural interest. Up to fifty children of each sex could be accommodated for a nominal charge of 5s each per week with apparently very favourable results. Ownership of the Yarrow Home passed to Westminster Hospital in 1947 and it remained under their control until around 1964, when it was purchased by Kent County Council to house Thanet Technical College. Grade II listed but now surplus to requirements, it may be converted into flats. (A. L.)

Thanet College, recently renamed East Kent College, has many modern buildings and a very attractive campus partly overlooking the sea. A great variety of courses are offered, including accountancy, hair dressing and catering. (A. L.)

The college's Bay Restaurant offers high-class cuisine to paying guests on most days in term time. Emphasising their keenness, first- and second-year students are here seen assembled together in the restaurant in May 2012. (A. L.)

Travelling along the coast from Broadstairs towards Ramsgate, Dumpton Gap is next encountered. Excepting central Ramsgate, it is the final breach in the almost continuous bastion of chalk cliffs which makes up the majority of the coastline of Thanet. Numerous substantial houses overlook the sea on the Ramsgate side of the Gap. (A. L.)

A little further westward lies the King George VI Memorial Park, originally the grounds of the stately East Cliff Lodge (*above*), which was built in about 1796–9 for Benjamin Hopkins. It had a number of owners, including Admiral Keith and, most notably, the Jewish philanthropist Sir Moses Montefiore, who bought it in 1831 and whose family remained there until 1935. It was occupied by the military during the war and, after passing to Thanet District Council, was demolished in 1954. (W. Cooke, *The Beauties of England and Wales*, 1805)

The gatehouse of East Cliff Lodge still survives, together with the stable block and greenhouse seen here, which has recently been restored. Grade II listed, it dates from the early nineteenth century. The curved design allows the maximum heat and light to penetrate the structure, which is largely of cast iron with fish-scale glass panes. (A. L.)

A short distance from the King George VI Park lies the attractive East Cliff Chine, which descends to the lower promenade. The same materials as employed for Madeira Walk here disguise the chalk to create a well-maintained rock garden that also provides a very pleasant place from which to view the sea. (A. L.)

ROUGH SEA, RAMSGATE

Approached by a long slope, Granville Parade has dwellings built into the cliff in a rather unusual way. While the houses remain, much has been lost from along this stretch, including the railway station on the sands (1863–1926), later Merrie England; the promenade pier; Marina Palace of Varieties; and large swimming baths.

One building of note that survives in this sea girt area was originally occupied by Lombardi, the photographers. Later it became the Marina restaurant. In recent years it has been enlarged and converted into apartments. (A. L)

Eastward along the East Cliff Promenade can be seen the St Cloud Hotel, later San Clu, which has partially survived to this day in modernised form as the Comfort Inn. At right the slope, seen earlier, leads down to the Marina Palace of Varieties, close to the two tollbooths at the entrance to the iron promenade pier. Just to the left of the St Cloud Hotel can be seen the distinctive terrace at the lower end of Albert Road, most probably designed by Edward Pugin.

The promenade pier, opened in 1881, was another victim of fire and general decay, leading to its demolition in 1930. However, the Marina Palace, with seating for 1,000 and serving a number of purposes as concert hall, ballroom, variety theatre and moving-picture house, fared better. It was extended as an attraction by the addition of a large swimming pool and boating lake, rather like the Lido at Cliftonville. This area is a car park today. (A. H. & S. Paragon Series)

The most prestigious hotel on the East Cliff was the Granville on Victoria Parade. It was designed by Edward Welby Pugin (1834–75) and built originally as a row of prestigious houses as part of his 'Gothic Revival'. Suffering considerable damage in the Second World War, it was later restored and converted into apartments.

Edward Pugin's memorial still stands in front of the Granville apartments, a perennial reminder of the influence he and his father had on the town. Another restored local facility is the lift, constructed in 1910, that descends from the East Cliff Promenade to the harbour, providing a more direct alternative to the artificial rockery of Madeira Walk. In Edwardian times there was a charge of 1d for its use, while today it is free, a most unusual occurrence. (A. L.)

This view from the steps adjacent to the lift captures various elements from different periods in time. The obelisk in the foreground commemorates King George IV's departure and return to Ramsgate in November 1821. He afterwards conferred the title 'Royal' on the harbour. Resting on the slipway is the Thames barge *Will*, formerly the *Will Everard*, sole survivor of the barges that brought coal to Margate over many years and referred to on page 27. Modern motor fishing boats bring the scene up to date. (A. L.)

Another reminder of times past in a modern setting. The replica of Captain Cook's barque *Endeavour* lies in the inner harbour marina at Ramsgate in the summer of 2000. The original 366-ton ship was a converted Whitby collier and it is interesting to note that the present vessel lies moored to the quay occupied by the regular colliers more than 120 years ago. (A. L.)

Important since 1835, numerous different craft have been repaired on Ramsgate's slipway. While the majority over the period 1920–60 were Watkins' tugs from the Thames, Trinity House has also occasionally brought tenders and lightships for repair and refitting. The Shipwright's Arms, right, and the domed Custom House of 1895 in Harbour Parade are here seen over the bow of light vessel No. 24. (A.L.)

This light vessel, No. 17, which had seen long service at the South Goodwin station, was brought to Ramsgate in January 2001 for refitting, repainting and preparation for conversion to solar power. (A. L.)

Two views showing different aspects of Ramsgate harbour in earlier days. This first shows the variety of vessels that used the harbour, including the ubiquitous Thames barge at centre rear, two brigantines and various wherries in the foreground, the latter mostly for hire to visitors. (Raphael Tuck & Sons)

This second illustration shows the passenger yachts being towed out by the paddle tug *Aid*. During the Edwardian years these were the *Champion*, *Prince Frederick William* and *Moss Rose*, the last-named later replaced by the *New Moss Rose*. They provided the same exhilarating or gut-wrenching experience as the yachts at Margate. (British Mirror Series)

The main entertainment attraction at the harbour was the Royal Victoria Pavilion, built at a cost of £40,000 and opened in June 1904 by HRH Princess Louise. The large hall, 130 feet long, could seat 2,000 people. At the time of construction it was decorated and upholstered in Louis XVI style. At either end of the hall were, 'octagons comprising tea rooms and buffets in the Adam style, with domed roofs, clustered columns and medallion paintings'. Today it is empty and faces an uncertain future. (Valentine's)

Harbour Parade was always busy in Edwardian times, with the ever-present trams and sailing ships. Beyond lies Royal Parade, completed in 1895, which climbs towards the West Cliff, while the original Military Road follows the edge of the harbour, allowing entry to the various workshops created beneath the slope. The view is essentially the same today, except the Royal Hotel was demolished and rebuilt further back from the road. (B. & R. Ltd.)

This view across the inner harbour towards Military Road shows a number of buildings of significance. At rear are the elegant Regency dwellings of Nelson Crescent with their delicate pagoda-style iron balconies. Furthest left on Military Road is the ice house of the Ramsgate Smack Owners Ice Company. Next come the steps of Jacob's Ladder, earlier built of timber, followed by the Sailors' church and the Smack Boys' Home, both institutions established by the Revd Eustace Brenan of Christ Church, who had concern for the physical and spiritual welfare of sailors in general and fishing smack apprentices in particular. (A. L.)

William Watkins' preserved tug *Cervia* provides a link with the harbour's past. Watkins took over the local engineering firm of Claxtons in 1920, their work of maintaining the fishing fleet having largely disappeared. In 1922 the firm completely rebuilt the *Hibernia* and then continued to regularly repair and refit the London tugs of Watkins, Gamecock Tugs and Elliott Steam Towage until 1960. (A. L.)

Ramsgate's fishing fleet did recover to some extent after the First World War, with steam drifters such as that in the foreground replacing the smacks. Various sailing smacks are also moored nearer to the Harbour Parade in this view from Military Road. The earlier Royal Hotel is prominent in this picture as well as the York Tea Rooms, Admiral Harvey pub and Crampton's Hotel. (Judges')

Despite the problems over the years an active fishing fleet still survives at Ramsgate, this modern motor vessel, *Holladays*, R8, providing an example of the twenty-five or so of under 10 metres that work from the outer harbour. Recently there has been a considerable increase in support craft for the large Thanet Offshore and London Array wind farms which also moor in the outer harbour. (A. L.)

Pleasure steamers were as popular at Ramsgate as Margate, although in the nineteenth century some more timid travellers would disembark at the latter place to avoid the sometimes turbulent passage around the North Foreland. This much later view shows the MV *Crested Eagle* (II) at the pier head in the summer of 1954 when this smaller vessel was based at Ramsgate. (Ramsgate Museum)

Larger in size, General Steam Navigation's *Queen of the Channel* lies moored in the same position ten years later. The introduction of 'no-passport' trips saw this last of GSN's fleet of sleek motor ships cross over to Boulogne for the first time in June 1956. Such was their popularity that the ship afterwards made regular summer sailings also to Calais and Dunkirk from Margate, Ramsgate and Deal for 40s. (£2) return until the service ended in 1966. (A. L.)

West Pier & Steamer, Ramsgate.

Trinity House, the authority responsible for many years for pilotage and the maintenance of coastal lights, had a depot at Ramsgate until 1914. The crosswall could be seen stacked with the various buoys of differing shapes and colours. In order to recover and replace the buoys, as well as service the local lightships, a tender was maintained at Ramsgate. *Alert* and *Triton* were two such vessels, but this appears to be the *Warden* of 1884. (L. & E. Skellet)

After 1914, lights maintenance was taken up by the Blackwall and Harwich depots. Pilotage passed to the various harbour authorities in 1988. At that time the boarding of pilots for the Thames and Medway was moved from Folkestone to Ramsgate and provided by Estuary Services Limited. Their new class of pilot launches brought a familiar name back to the port, with the *Estuary Warden* seen here entering the harbour in 1996. (A. L.)

Modern cross-Channel ferries only started operating continuously from Ramsgate after the enlarged harbour had been completed in 1983–4. Initial operators Schiaffino Freight Ferries merged in July 1990 with Sally (UK) Holdings Group, owners of the passenger ferries. Their vessels sailing between 1981 and 1998 to Dunkirk included *The Viking*, *Sally Star* and *Sally Sky*. Most popular was *Sally Star*, seen here approaching Ramsgate just before her withdrawal in April 1997. Currently, TransEuropa Ferries operate a service to Ostend. (A. L.)

The east pier at Ramsgate makes for a pleasant stroll on a bracing day, with often a variety of ferries, ships and boats to add interest. A scene of much activity in the past, pleasure steamers no longer call at the pier head. In their day the Sun Café occupied the first floor of the adjacent building, later renamed the Eagle Café, where diners could enjoy a most impressive view of the sea and harbour. Sadly it was closed some years ago. (A. L.)

Beyond the new Port Ramsgate area the Western Undercliff is reached, which earlier afforded a tranquil spot with seats and shelters. This short promenade was later extended for a considerable distance in the direction of Pegwell. In an attempt perhaps to enliven the sleepy resort, in the sixties a new purpose was found for this lower promenade – a series of standing-start quarter-mile trials. (E. A. Sweetman & Sons, Sologlaze Series)

Motorcyclists arrived in hordes for these events and for their duration the undercliff promenade was no longer tranquil as Vincent 500 and 1000 machines, left, were wound up to full throttle. Safety considerations would rule against such an event nowadays, for the railings were not exactly forgiving. The Ramsgate end of this promenade became part of the port approach road, seen at right, when the new access tunnel was built. (A. L.)

There is also a wide promenade on the top of the West Cliff and where the Paragon ends there once stood this bandstand, in sunken Italian Gardens with 'prim steps and slopes and square-cut beds'. It was replaced in 1914 by the West Cliff Hall, a building similar to Margate's Winter Gardens, which later became a motor museum; so are the interests of different generations satisfied. At the moment it is overgrown and between uses. (Valentine's)

Constructed in a piecemeal way over the years 1820–45, the adjoining Royal Crescent has survived and has been recently restored. It is viewed here from the top of the West Cliff Hall, which forms part of the promenade. In contrast to its companion the Wellington Crescent on the East Cliff, it has the better position as the main road runs at the rear and the sea views are undisturbed. The garden of West Cliff Lodge beyond was the site of the model village between 1953 and 2003. (A. L.)

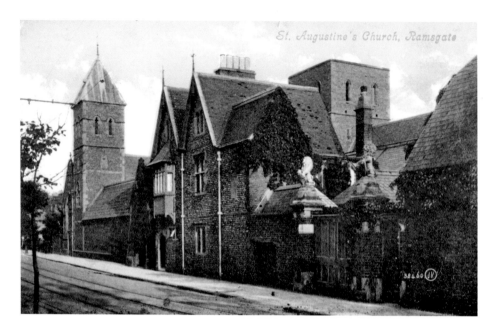

Just beyond Royal Crescent lies St Augustine's Roman Catholic church. Designed by Augustus Pugin and commenced in 1846, it is a masterpiece of flint with dressings of Whitby stone. The interior is richly decorated with paintings and carvings and the large font with its ornate cover was thought to have been intended for a grander edifice. On the opposite side of St Augustine's Road, a Benedictine monastery was completed in the same style by Pugin's son Edward but the monks have now left that residence and it is up for sale. (Valentine's)

The fourteen Stations of the Cross in St Augustine's church, showing Christ's crucifixion in striking relief, were made of terracotta in Belgium by de Beule of Ghent in 1893 and painted in the 1960s. Pilgrims are being encouraged to visit this Catholic shrine to St Augustine, who landed in Thanet in AD 597. A major restoration of the church is also taking place. (A. L.)

Augustus Welby Pugin (1812–52) came to Ramsgate in 1843, building his house The Grange in the Gothic style by 1845. It was designed as an ornate family home harking back to the Middle Ages, having a private chapel and a distinctive tower. He produced much of his finest work in the library here, creating designs at great speed, but was only forty when he died. (A. L.)

A stark contrast to Pugin's work can be seen in the Art Deco Ramsgate Airport terminal building. Initially considered during the First World War, the 90-acre field was in use in July 1935 and the above building was opened by Sir Francis Shelmerdine, Director-General of Civil Aviation, in 1937. Sadly, Ramsgate Airport closed in 1968 and the derelict terminal was later demolished.

Private flying was also popular at Ramsgate, the Thanet Aero Club being formed in March 1936. Unfortunately, a light aircraft belonging to the club crashed into the sea off Cliftonville in July 1938 while carrying out aerobatics above HMS *Revenge*, occupants Edmund Betts and Marjorie Walk being killed. In post-war years the field was devoted largely to private flying, with Auster Autocrats, Miles Messengers, Percival Proctors and DH Tiger Moths as regular visitors.

After its official reopening in June 1953, pleasure flights to view the coastal resorts were offered by three de Havilland Dragon Rapides of Island Air Services. Unfortunately one of their aircraft, G-AGUF, crashed on take-off on a trip on 29 June 1957 and was written off, although all the passengers escaped safely. This caused the service to be curtailed. A year or so earlier a Tiger Moth had crash landed at the airport after hitting the top of one of the aerial masts of the nearby North Foreland Radio Station. That aircraft was also dismantled. (A. L.)

Although not a front-line Battle of Britain aerodrome, RAF Manston had a lengthy wartime involvement, providing a base for squadrons of Hawker Typhoons. Mk XVI Spitfire TB 752 was retained as a gate guardian after the war and it was eventually set aside as a memorial in the sixties, to be later accompanied by a Canberra and Gloster Javelin. (A. L.)

Such was the interest in the Spitfire that it was totally rebuilt in the seventies and this special building constructed to house it in 1981. In 1988 it was much enlarged to accommodate a Hawker Hurricane as well and much associated material was collected to form the present Spitfire and Hurricane Memorial Museum. The adjoining Merlin Café is additionally a pleasant place to enjoy light lunches and teas with home-made cakes.(A. L.)

In 1950 Manston was transferred to the United States Air Force (USAF) for use as a base for F-84 Thunderjets, Thunderstreaks and F-86 Sabre fighters. There was also a range of support aircraft including Grumman Albatross amphibians and Sikorsky S.55 helicopters for air-sea rescue work. Thunderjets (*above*) were not universally reliable, one in particular crashing on a bank in St Peters in April 1952, killing the pilot and three residents.

The USAF left Manston in 1958 and the base was handed back to the RAF. After that the station became a Major Diversionary Airfield, providing emergency landing arrangements for aircraft in difficulties. There were still reminders of the past, however, for in 1963 a group of B-17 Flying Fortresses arrived to participate in the making of the film *The War Lover*. (A. L.)

Although a military aerodrome, civilian flights were permitted at Manston from the late fifties. Initial players were Invicta Airways and Air Ferry. The former flew to a number of the new holiday destinations in Spain and Yugoslavia. This Douglas Skymaster of Invicta carried eighty-four passengers in the mid-sixties. (Invicta Airways)

One important activity carried out at Manston since 1958 is the training of firefighters. This organisation progressed to become the prestigious Fire Services Central Training Establishment, with the particular speciality of fighting aircraft fires, latterly the Defence Fire Training and Development Centre. Some exercises on obsolete aircraft are often noticeable by the large palls of smoke generated.

Probably the most gallant action carried out from Manston was Operation Fuller, the attack by Swordfish torpedo bombers of 825 Naval Air Squadron led by Lt-Commander Eugene Esmonde against the German battleships *Scharnhorst* and *Gneisenau* during their 'Channel Dash' of 12 February 1942. Esmonde and many of the other naval airmen were killed. He was awarded a posthumous Victoria Cross for his courage. This recently installed memorial lies outside the Clock House on Ramsgate Harbour. (A. L.)

RAF Manston closed on 31 March 1999, becoming Kent International Airport. EU-Jet subsequently flew to a large number of European destinations, too many, as it turned out, to be financially viable. In recent years Flybe ran a regular service to Edinburgh but that also has closed, leaving the main operators as cargo carriers. While new developments are awaited, a number of time-expired aircraft are stored at Manston awaiting disposal, including several Boeing 747s. (A. L.)

86

Returning to the sea, Pegwell Bay, the last bay of Thanet, has retained its quiet backwater appearance in this Victorian view which shows in the background Court Stairs with their jetty, and that which served the Belle Vue Hotel from around 1784. These were replaced by a new pier by 1879 as part of the reclamation project of 6 acres of foreshore to create the Ravenscliff Gardens. Tatnell's Clifton Tavern and Tea Gardens on the left were replaced by the convalescent home. (H. & J. West)

Pegwell village seen in Edwardian times. At left is the Belle Vue Tavern, dating from around 1797 and serving, according to Dickens, 'small saucers of large shrimps, dabs of butter, crusty loaves and bottled ale. The finest shrimps I ever saw were caught here.' Their popularity is borne out by Samuel Banger's Original Essence and Potted Shrimp Factory on the right-hand side of the street. The more recent but short-lived building in the background whose far side overlooked the now-derelict Ravenscliff Gardens has a sign for a rifle club, which may have formed part of the lower gardens. (Welch & Sons)

PEGWELL BAY

REGATTA

PATRONESS.

Her Royal Highness the Duchess of Kent.

PATRONS

His Grace the Duke of Buccleuch	RT. Hon. & Rev. Earl Guilford.
Rt. Hon. Lord Sondes	Sir John Rae Reid, Bart. M.P.
Rt. Hon. Lord A. Conyngham, M.P.	E. R. Rice Esq. M.P.
Rt. Hon. Sir E. Knatchbull, Bart. M.P.	Sir Brook W. Bridges, Bart.
Rt. Hon. S. R. Lushington	J.A. Warre Esq.
Honorable Richard Watson	J. P. Powell Esq.

THE BOATS TO START AT ONE O'CLOCK PRECISELY.

The Nobility, Gentry, Visitors and the Public are most respectfully informed that the **ELEVENTH ANNUAL REGATTA** will take place on

TUESDAY, the 5th of September, 1837;

ON WHICH OCCASION THERE WILL BE

Three Silver Cups!

AND OTHER PRIZES.

First Race,-Four Oared Galleys,
FOR THE

Royal Victoria Cup:

The Cup is open to competition for FOUR OARED FIR or other Built, REGATTA GALLEYS, from any Town or Place on the Kentish Coast, not to exceed 29 feet. Three boats to start or no Race.

Second Race, Six Oared Galleys:
FOR THE

Royal Kent Cup:

This cup is open to competition for SIX OARED FIR or other built REGATTA GALLEYS, not exceeding 32ft 6in. from any town or place on the Kentish Coast. Three boats to start or no Race.

Third Race, Six Oared Galleys:
FOR THE

SONDES CUP:

The Cup is open to competition for SIX OARED SERVICE GALLEYS not exceeding 31 feet, from any part of the Kentish Coast. Fir built boats ——— to enter in the Race. Three boats to start or no Race.

A ROWING MATCH,

IN SKIFFS:

By Young Men under the age of Eighteen ———

The Value of the Prizes will be duly announced, and all other Particulars in future Bills.

The Prizes in the above classes will be open for competition to all persons having the above description of Boats on their being properly entered and the Entrance Money (five shillings) paid on or before Tuesday, the 29th of August. All Boats entered after that day to pay double entrance. Competitors are eligible to contest at this Regatta FROM ANY PART OF THE KENTISH COAST, from Whitstable to Sandgate.——the Committee to decide on the eligibility of the respective Boats for Entrance. After the Regatta is concluded there will be a

Rustic Fete on the Sands:

BALLOONS WILL ASCEND, and

IN THE EVENING A BRILLIANT DISPLAY OF FIRE WORKS.

It is particularly requested that all persons having Boats to enter will immediately announce the name. Gentlemen ——— conforming to the Regulations. Communications relative to the Regatta to be addressed to the Stewards, or to John S. CRAMP, Belle Vue Terrace, Pegwell Bay.

Should the Weather prove unfavourable the Regatta will take place on the following or next fine day after.

SUBSCRIPTIONS are currently Solicited, and received at the Banks of Messrs. Austen & Co. and Messrs. Burgess & Co., at Messrs. Sackett and Fuller's Workers Library and at B.T. Jarman's, Albion Hill, RAMSGATE; Bettisons Libraries MARGATE; Hale's Library BROADSTAIRS and by J.S. Cramp, Pegwell Bay.

B.T.JARMAN, PRINTER & BOOKSELLER, ALBION HILL, RAMSGATE

Pegwell Bay was obviously well known to those with discerning tastes at an early date, as shown by those supporting the local regatta in 1837. Apparently the Duchess of Kent and Princess Victoria came to sample the shrimp teas in 1831, and six years later, only a month after the date of this regatta, John Cramp of the Belle Vue inn was granted a royal appointment as Purveyor of Essence of Shrimps in Ordinary to Her Majesty the Queen.

Along with others such as Alfred Yarrow, the Working Men's Club and Institute Union were seeking a site for a convalescent home. The derelict Clifton Tavern was selected and the distinctive building above declared open on the stormy August Bank Holiday of 1894. Initially it accommodated thirty-two residents but was later extended. Tommy Skidmore from Sheffield occupied the room at right marked with an 'X' for the Christmas of 1924. (Photochrom Co.)

A distinctive and attractive building, the former convalescent home in Pegwell Road is now the very comfortable Pegwell Bay Hotel, with forty-two en-suite rooms. (A. L.)

This very different view from desolate Shell Ness at the mouth of the River Stour shows how the shallow waters of Pegwell Bay and also open fields nearby were defended against invasion in the last war. This computer-generated image shows only a few of the many poles that were embedded in the sand to discourage a landing by German troops. (A. L.)

The same section of cliffs viewed from the head of the bay show them to be one of the few undeveloped sections of this coastline. Quieter since the Hoverport closed, the shore area, reclaimed over the years by large amounts of Spartina grass, has become a nature reserve. (A. L.)

The main attraction of Pegwell Bay is the *Hugin*, a replica of a Viking ship of around AD 890 that was presented to the United Kingdom as a gesture of goodwill by Prince Georg of Denmark, acknowledging the assistance given to his country in the Second World War. A crew of fifty-three Danes sailed and rowed the longship from Esbjerg, Denmark, in the traditional way, to arrive off east Kent on 27 July 1949. After spending the night moored alongside the North Goodwin lightship, the *Hugin* was piloted into Main Bay, Broadstairs, the following day by local boatman Douglas Kirkaldie. A huge crowd had assembled for this event, which commemorated the landing of the Jutish chieftains Hengist and Horsa 1,500 years earlier at Ebbsfleet, near Ramsgate. The ship's crew subsequently went to that place to celebrate the meeting of their fifth-century ancestors with King Vortigern of Kent and his subsequent betrothal to Rowena, Hengist's daughter.

The *Hugin*, named after one of Odin's ravens, was built of Danish oak with copper nails at Frederikssund from drawings in the Danish Maritime Museum, but largely resembles the Norwegian Gokstad ship. The 15-ton vessel is 71 feet in length, 18 feet in the beam and has a depth of 6 feet. The height of the mast is 40 feet and the sail area 430 square feet.

Following the arrival of the *Hugin*, Main Bay in Broadstairs was renamed Viking Bay. The ship itself was purchased by the *Daily Mail* newspaper and made a tour of various ports and a trip up the Thames to Greenwich and Richmond. Afterwards, it was placed on a permanent site at Pegwell Bay near to the point of the original landing in AD 449. (Sunbeam Photo Ltd)

The *Hugin* in the position on the extensive lawns that it has occupied since 1949. Having suffered from exposure to the elements for more than fifty years, the ship was given a full restoration in 2005. (A. L.)

Not so fortunate was St Augustine's Hotel, which stood opposite the site chosen for the *Hugin*, and which subsequently profited from its name as the Viking Ship Motel and Restaurant, selling Truman's Beers. The building of the Hoverport also worked in its favour but the closure of the same had a detrimental effect. Later demolished, the area is now occupied by Courtland Close. (Sunbeam Photo Ltd.)

Hoverlloyd's experimental introduction of the thirty-six-seat SRN-6 hovercraft for Channel crossings commenced from Ramsgate Harbour in April 1966, with a fare of £4 10s (£4.50) charged for the return trip. Named *Swift* and *Sure*, these two craft proved that a viable service was possible and a decision was made to build the world's first international hoverport at Pegwell Bay. Some 300,000 tons of colliery shale was used for the foundations. (A. L.)

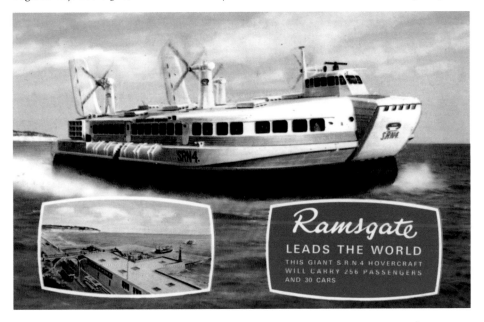

The larger SRN-4 hovercraft shown in British Hovercraft Corporation livery was first evaluated at Pegwell Bay. There were great hopes for this service and, despite complaints about the noise and concerns from bait diggers, it was immediately successful, the time for crossing the Channel being shortened to forty minutes in reasonable weather. (E. T. W. Dennis and Sons)

The later SRN-4 *Swift*, seen in Hoverlloyd colours at Pegwell Bay around 1970. Although visibility was limited, their cruising speed of 45 knots gave an exhilarating impression to those used to the regular cross-Channel steamers. The route usually followed the Goodwin Sands, that previous wrecker of ships, giving a smooth passage over the first stages, but leaving the southern end gave you quite a jolt if there was any kind of sea running. (E. T. W. Dennis)

Captain Bill Williamson, left, was one of those who started the Hoverlloyd service. Others were Tom Wilson, Roy Mortlock and George Kennedy. Leslie Colquhoun was managing director. Pegwell Bay Hoverport was opened in May 1969 by the Duke of Edinburgh. The view from the control cabin of an SRN-4 hovercraft in mid-Channel is seen at right. (A. L.)

In 1978, 233,000 cars passed through Pegwell Bay together with 1,266,000 passengers, with departures every thirty minutes between 6 a.m. and 8 p.m. However, the merger of Hoverlloyd and Seaspeed led to all operations moving to Dover by the summer of 1982. Later returned to Thanet Council, no further use was found for the site and it became derelict; the sad end of a local success story. (A. L.)

Richborough power station was built on part of the site of the famous 'Mystery Port' of the First World War. Completed around 1962, this 360-megawatt station was intended to burn coal from the Kentish fields but this was not successful and oil had to be added to improve combustion. Eventually converted to burn Orimulsion from South America, pollution problems led to its final closure. This landmark stood derelict for more than fifteen years before the chimney and cooling towers were blown up early in 2012. (A. L.)

Acknowledgements

After my parents moved to Cliftonville in 1946, I attended various private schools close to home and at Birchington and latterly Charles Dickens School, Broadstairs, on its opening in 1955. Initially employed by Pfizers at Sandwich in 1959, I remained in Thanet until 1965 when I left to study chemistry at university. My parents, however, remained in Cliftonville until 1977. Drawn back to my roots after retiring in 1996, my wife and I left Oxfordshire to buy a house at Whitfield, near Dover, where I could still keep in touch with the Isle of Thanet.

This book represents a nostalgic trip through the past century or so, years which have seen mixed fortunes for the Thanet towns and great changes in some areas. As I am conscious that a book of this size can only offer a very limited coverage of these changes, I feel it is important to list some of the more detailed accounts that have been published about the island. Earliest is by the Revd John Lewis, entitled *History and Antiquities of the Isle of Tenet* (1736). Edward Hasted also gives a good account in the tenth volume of his *History and Topographical Survey of the County of Kent* (c. 1797). There are many illustrated guides that describe the towns in detail after 1815 and I have gained much information from the Ward Lock *Pictorial and Descriptive Guides to Margate and North-East Kent* and *Kelly's Street Directories* of 1900–70. More recent details rely to a large extent on my recollections but where these have become vague, I have been fortunate in receiving considerable help from local citizens with long, unbroken memories of the towns.

Mick Twyman.

I mention firstly the late Mick Twyman, who studied Margate's history in great depth and investigated many local sites, particularly the origin of the Tudor House. In doing so he amassed a collection of more than 5,000 postcards and photographs of the town. Mick's collection was scanned for posterity and I here record my sincere thanks to his widow, Eve, for allowing me to use pictures from his collection. These particular examples are acknowledged as M. T. collection. Wherever possible I have tried to acknowledge the original source of the pictures but here apologise for any errors or omissions on that score. My photographs bear my own initials.

Beyond Margate, I thank Michael Hunt, a resident of Broadstairs, but previously curator of Ramsgate Maritime Museum, for help with the history of both those towns and for access to his work, *A History of Ramsgate Harbour & Guide to its Existing Features* (2007). Equally, I express my gratitude to John Williams of Margate Museum for assistance with subjects maritime within the town and aeronautical as far afield as Manston aerodrome.

I also extend my special thanks to Chris Sandwell, whose family has a very long association with Margate, and particularly with the lifeboat. Chris, in his shore-side role of postman, has delivered to every known address in the greater Margate area during his thirty-five years with the Post Office. His experiences and interest in local history have been of invaluable help in ensuring that this account is as accurate as possible.

There have been many others who have helped: various internet websites, like Thanet Earth; eBay sellers who provided postcards; staff at Birchington Heritage Centre and the two Manston RAF museums; and finally those who have stopped for a chat and supplied me with information as I strolled by. I hope that all who read this book may enjoy it as much as I have its preparation.